CARNIVORE DIET

28 day Meal Plan, Step by step process, Fun & Engaging

Table of Content

Introduction 1

Week 1 8
Getting Started 8

Day 1 10
Beef Liver and Eggs Scramble 10
Bone Broth with Beef Slices 10
Grilled Chicken Thighs with Butter 11

Day 2 12
Pork Belly Slices and Scrambled Eggs 12
Lamb Chops with Bone Marrow Butter 12
Grass-fed Steak with Garlic Butter 13

Day 3 14
Beef Sausages with Fried Eggs 14
Chicken Wings with Hot Sauce 14
Salmon Filet with Lemon Butter 15

Day 4 16
Beef and Egg Patty 16
Pork Ribs 16
Tuna Steaks with Olive Oil Drizzle 17

Day 5 18
Beef Bacon and Boiled Eggs 18
Turkey Drumsticks 18
Sardines in Olive Oil 19

Day 6 20
Ground Beef with Eggs 20
Chicken Breast with Herb Butter 20
Trout with Clarified Butter 21

Day 7 22
Lamb Sausages with Poached Eggs 22
Bone-in Ribeye Steak 22
Grilled Shrimp with Lime Butter 23

Why Week 1 is Crucial 24

Week 2 26
Day 8 28
Venison Patties with Eggs 28
Swordfish with Garlic Butter 28
Duck Breast with Orange Reduction 29

Day 9 30
Bone Marrow with Toasted Liver Pâté 30
Beef Brisket 30
Lobster Tail with Drawn Butter 31

Day 10 32
Ground Bison and Eggs Scramble 32

Mackerel with Olive Oil 32

Roast Chicken Leg Quarter 33

Day 11 34
Pork Sausage with Fried Eggs 34

Roast Leg of Lamb 35

Beef Meatballs 35

Day 12 36
Ground Turkey and Egg Patty 36

Salmon Roe with Cream Cheese 36

Beef Tenderloin with Herb Butter 37

Day 13 38
Beef Jerky with Boiled Eggs 38

Smoked Pork Shoulder 38

Grilled Calamari with Olive Oil 39

Day 14 40
Chorizo with Scrambled Eggs 40

Venison Roast 40

Chicken Livers with Butter 41

Week 2:   Nourish and Flourish- Embracing the Nutrient Beats 42

Week 3 43
Day 15 45

Pork Loin and Eggs 45

Slow-Cooked Beef Stew 45

Baked Cod with Lemon Butter 46

Day 16 47

Ground Lamb with Poached Eggs 47

Grilled Herring with Olive Oil 47

Beef Short Ribs 48

Day 17 49

Beef Tongue Slices with Eggs 49

Rabbit Stew 49

Trout Almandine with Butter 50

Day 18 51

Prosciutto with Fried Eggs 51

Grilled Octopus with Lemon Olive Oil 51

Osso Buco 52

Day 19 53

Beef Pastrami and Eggs 53

Bison Steak 53

Oysters with Lemon Juice 54

Day 20 55
Ground Chicken and Egg Patty 55
Sardines with Garlic Butter 55
Pork Tenderloin 56

Day 21 57
Beef Salami with Scrambled Eggs 57
Canned Tuna in Olive Oil 57
Roast Duck Leg 58

Week 3: End of Week Reflection- Renew and Rejoice - The Refreshing Remix 59

Week 4 60
Day 22 61
Elk Patties with Eggs 61
Lobster Bisque 61
Beef T-bone Steak 62

Day 23 63
Ground Veal and Eggs 63
Slow-Cooked Pork Belly 63
Grilled Eel with Butter 64

Day 24 65
Beef Hot Dogs with Scrambled Eggs 65
Grilled Goose Breast 65
Mussels in Garlic Butter 66

Day 25...67
Beef Ham and Eggs... 67
Clams with Lemon Butter... 67
Roasted Quail... 68

Day 26...69
Ground Pork and Poached Eggs.................................... 69
Lamb Shoulder Roast... 69
Grilled Tilapia with Olive Oil.................................. 70

Day 27... 71
Duck Egg Omelette with Beef Strips...............................71
Grilled Lamb Koftas..71
Pan-Seared Tuna with Butter Sauce............................... 72

Day 28...73
Veal Sausages with Eggs... 73
Beef Prime Rib.. 73
Scallops with Butter and Lemon.................................. 74

Your 28-Day Carnivorous Chronicle............................ 76
Ancient Appetites:... 78
Counterculture and Curiosity:................................ 79

INTRODUCTION

Embark on a 28-day journey that pays homage to the primal allure of the carnivore diet. In a world teeming with dietary choices, this book elevates the meaty classics, placing them center stage. Here, we champion the nutrient-packed, flavor-rich symphony of animal-based foods. From insightful narratives, curated meal plans, to trackers that ensure your holistic well-being, this book is your ultimate guide to embracing the carnivore lifestyle.

From steak symphonies to bacon ballads, let's tune into nature's nutrient-rich playlist and discover a harmony that resonates deeply with our primal selves.

Have you ever felt the sheer joy of biting into a perfectly grilled steak or the comfort that a hearty beef stew brings on a chilly evening? If yes, you're about to embark on a journey that celebrates those very emotions, every single day for 28 days.

In the pages that follow, you'll uncover the essence of the carnivore diet, not just as a nutritional path, but as a lifestyle, a philosophy. A diet that's not merely about cutting out certain foods but embracing a richer, fuller plate. Alongside this delectable journey, we'll also be your compass, guiding you through the myriad of changes your body will experience, ensuring you understand and thrive through each phase.

We've curated an experience that encompasses the beauty of animal-based foods, educates on its myriad benefits, guides through cost-effective practices, and provides tools to track your personal and transformational journey. So, as you flip through, remember, it's not just a diet plan you hold in your hands, but a celebration of nature's finest, waiting to be relished.
Embrace the carnivore within and let the transformation begin!

What: The Meat of the Matter
"Imagine if life was as straightforward as a burger - the juicy, meaty patty being the star of the show, stealing all the limelight from the lettuce and tomatoes."
That's the carnivore diet in a "meatball"! In this diet, we're focusing primarily on animal-based foods. Think of it like being at a concert where the meats are the rockstars and veggies are, well, backstage. Meat isn't just about taste, it's nutrient-rich too! For instance, did you know that beef liver is one of the most nutrient-dense foods on the planet? It's packed with Vitamin A, Folate, and Iron. Talk about a superfood, but in meat form!

How: The Butcher's Guide to Going Carnivore
"Do you remember playing 'Connect the Dots' as a kid? Well, going carnivore is kind of like that."
Instead of bouncing from broccoli to beetroot, you're gliding from steak to salmon. It's a journey, but not the kind that requires a map. Just a fork and a knife! Fun fact: Over the past two decades, there's been a whopping 500% increase in the number of people going for meat-centric diets. That's half the globe wanting their steak and eating it too!

Why: Beyond the Sizzle and Steak
"Picture this: You're in a fancy car (James Bond-level fancy), but instead of putting premium fuel in, you opt for the not-so-good stuff."
You see, our bodies can be like those luxury cars. The carnivore diet is all about giving our bodies the premium fuel they deserve. Quality proteins and fats found in meats play a crucial role in muscle repair, hormone production, and even mood regulation. In 2019, a survey revealed that 62% of carnivore diet followers felt an increase in energy and mood stability. That's a majority of people riding the meaty wave to happier shores!

The Individual Symphony: Why One Diet Doesn't Conduct Every Orchestra

"Think of our bodies as a collection of musical instruments – while they may all belong to the orchestra, each has its unique sound and needs. Now, imagine trying to tune a flute the same way as a cello. Sounds absurd, right?"
In the world of nutrition, there's no universal remote. What makes one person dance might make another snooze. Here's why the carnivore diet might not strike the right chord for everyone:

The Genetic Playlist: Just like how some of us can roll our tongues and some can't, our genes play a massive role in determining how we respond to different diets. Your DNA might be more suited to a mix of veggies and meats, while your best friend's might shout 'encore!' on a full carnivore menu.

Tuning the Gut: Our gut is home to billions of bacteria that have their own dietary preferences. Some guts might throw a party with meat, while others might prefer a more diverse buffet. These tiny critters influence everything from digestion to mood. So, if the carnivore diet doesn't seem to be in harmony with your gut, it might be your microbiome asking for a different tune.

Life's Rhythms: Our activity levels, stress, sleep patterns, and even our environment play a part in how a diet affects us. An athlete with rigorous training might have different protein needs compared to someone leading a sedentary lifestyle.

Past Concerts: Previous diets, health conditions, and even medications can influence how your body responds to a new diet. If you've been a vegetarian for 15 years and suddenly jump onto the carnivore wagon, your body might hit a few off-notes before getting into the groove.

The key takeaway? It's essential to listen to your body's symphony. If something feels off-key, it might be time to rejig the composition. Remember, the goal isn't to follow a trend but to find what makes your body play its best music!

"Meat" the Benefits: Why Going Carnivore Could Have You Roaring with Delight!
"Imagine becoming a superhero overnight! While the carnivore diet won't exactly give you the ability to fly (unless you count feeling lighter!), it does come with a cape-full of perks. Here's what you might experience:"

Less Noise in the Kitchen: Eating carnivore is like having a playlist with only your favorite songs. No more juggling between dozens of ingredients or long recipe lists. It's simple, straightforward, and cuts out the culinary cacophony!

Unleashing the Protein Power: Meat is a powerhouse of protein. And what does protein do? Think of it as the gym instructor for your muscles. It helps repair, maintain, and grow those biceps and triceps, ensuring you're flex-ready anytime.

Fat: The Unsung Hero: On the carnivore diet, fat isn't the villain; it's the star of the show! Consuming more fats can provide sustained energy, making you feel like the Energizer bunny. Plus, fats play a vital role in hormone production. Talk about a behind-the-scenes MVP!

Kiss Those Sugar Crashes Goodbye: By cutting out carbs, you're essentially removing the rollercoaster of blood sugar spikes and crashes. The result? A more steady energy level and fewer mid-afternoon slumps.

A Digestive Holiday: For some, giving the greens a break can actually be a digestive delight. Without fibrous veggies, some folks find their stomachs singing a happier, less gassy tune.

Mental Clarity: Some carnivore converts report a clearer mind, sharper focus, and better concentration. It's like upgrading your brain to 5G while everyone else is still on dial-up.

Glowing Reviews for Your Skin: Got pesky pimples? The carnivore diet might just be the beauty regime you've been looking for. Anecdotal reports suggest clearer skin after ditching plant-based foods.

Remember, while these are potential benefits, everyone's body jams to its own tune. So, while you might be headbanging to the carnivore beat, your friend might be swaying to a different rhythm. The key is to find what makes your body feel like a rockstar!

The Quest for Quality Meat: A Carnivore's Compass

So, you've decided to embark on the carnivore diet adventure. Huzzah! But, before you go sharpening your cutlery, there's a crucial topic to sink our teeth into - the quality of your meat. It's the crux of the diet, so ensuring its top-notch is pivotal.

The Prime Importance of Quality Meat

Meat isn't just meat. It's a tapestry of flavors, nutrients, and textures. The better the quality, the better it is for your body and your taste buds. Here's why:

Nutrient Density: Premium quality meat typically has a higher concentration of vitamins, minerals, and beneficial fatty acids.

Fewer Additives: Quality meat tends to have fewer antibiotics, hormones, and other unwanted additives.

Ethical Considerations: Higher quality often means better animal welfare standards. It's a win-win; good for the soul and the palate!

Navigating the Supermarket Safari

Become a Meat Detective: Like Sherlock with a shopping cart, you must deduce which meat is suitable.

Check the Labels: Look for terms like "grass-fed", "organic", and "pasture-raised". These usually indicate a higher quality product.

Ingredient Intrigue: For processed meats (like sausages), check the ingredients. Avoid those with sugar, grains, fillers, or excessive preservatives. For example, a good sausage might simply have pork, water, salt, and natural spices.

Color Commentary: Fresh meat should have a vibrant, natural color. Bright red for beef, pink for pork, etc. Browning could indicate age.

Online Outlets for Quality Cuts

While we're not sponsored or affiliated, many carnivores swear by these online sources:
USA: ButcherBox - Offers a curated selection of high-quality meats, right to your door. They emphasize grass-fed beef, free-range organic chicken, and heritage-breed pork.
UK: Farmison & Co - A heralded provider of British heritage meats, focusing on breed diversity and ethical farming.
Australia: The Meat Club - They take pride in their pasture-fed, hormone-free, and antibiotic-free meats. Their Angus beef is especially noteworthy.
In essence, when it comes to meat on the carnivore diet, it's not just about quantity but quality. It's about choosing cuts that not only tantalize the taste buds but also nourish the body. Happy hunting! 🥩🔍🛒

Portion Proportions: Tailoring Your Tasty Tidbits

Eating is a lot like dressing up. Just as you wouldn't throw on any old piece of clothing without checking the fit, when it comes to food, it's about finding the 'just right' portion that complements your body. And remember, while guidelines are helpful, they're just starting points on this culinary journey. Tailoring is the secret ingredient.

Our Recipe Baseline

Our recipes start with a certain 'cut' or size in mind, designed for:
Men: Aimed at someone standing around 5'9" (175cm) tall and weighing about 155-165 pounds (70-75kg).
Women: Catered to an individual approximately 5'4" (162.5cm) in height and weighing around 120-130 pounds (54-59kg).
But, here's the thing: humans aren't cookie-cutter figures. This means our 'one-size' is a mere guideline. Let's dive into the adjustments.

Tailoring for Your Unique Fit

For Larger Men & Women: If you're a gentleman taller than 6'2" (188cm) or a lady above 5'9" (175cm), or if either of you possesses a more robust frame, consider beefing up (pun intended) the portions by about 25-30%.

For Smaller Men & Women: Men below 5'7" (170cm) or women under 5'2" (157.5cm) might want to trim down the portions by 15-20%. That steak in the recipe might need a little downsizing.

Activity Levels Matter: Whether you're a marathon runner, a yoga enthusiast, or someone who loves a good Netflix binge, your activity levels play a role. Those burning more calories might need more fuel. Those on the more sedentary side? Perhaps a little less.

Finding Your Perfect Serving Size

These are just signposts on your carnivore journey. Listen to your body. It'll give you cues. Hungry often? Maybe up those portions a tad. Feeling too full or seeing undesired weight changes? Consider scaling back. Starting with our guidelines, adjust over a week, note how you feel, and then make more changes if necessary. It's a bit of trial and error, a sprinkle of intuition, and a dollop of self-awareness. Remember, this diet, like any good outfit, should fit you perfectly, not the other way around.

WEEK 1

GETTING STARTED

Adapting to a Meat Dominant Diet

"Imagine if our ancestors had meal delivery services or takeaway options like 'UberEats Mammoth Deluxe'? Nope, they dined au naturel, and we're going back to those roots (minus the mammoths!). Welcome to Week 1!"

Let's face it: Change can be as tough as a well-done steak if you're not prepared. But here's your marinating guide to soften the blow. As you embark on this carnivore journey, you're not just starting a diet; you're embarking on a culinary adventure! Think of this week as the "warm-up" before the big concert. We're tuning our instruments (or, in this case, our kitchen and habits) and getting ready for the main show.

Why Week 1 is Crucial:

If you've been a carb-cuddler or a sugar-snuggler for most of your life, diving straight into the deep end of the carnivore pool can feel a tad cold. It's not just about switching foods; it's a holistic shift in how you view nutrition. Week 1 is about setting the stage, prepping your mindset, and becoming familiar with your new food pals.

Adjusting Your Palate:

You might suddenly realize how sweet a tomato can taste or how beef has different flavor notes. As you reduce and remove other foods, you become a connoisseur of meats. Steak isn't just steak anymore - it's a symphony of tastes!

Getting Over the Carb Hump:

The first week might see you battling the infamous 'low-carb flu' as your body waves goodbye to glucose and turns to fat for fuel. It's like switching from regular fuel to premium in your car. There might be a few sputters and stalls, but soon enough, you'll be revving smoothly.

Meat: Your New BFF:

Meat is more than just the main course in this diet; it's your partner in crime, your culinary confidant. Learning its many forms – from steaks to broths – will be essential. This week is about exploring the range and recognizing quality.

In conclusion, this isn't just about eating. It's an experience, a throwback, and a challenge all rolled into one. By the end of this week, you'll have a deeper understanding and appreciation for the path you've chosen. So, sharpen those knives and set your tables; it's time to dine like our ancestors – with flair, fun, and a whole lot of meat!

DAY 1

☀️ **BREAKFAST**   ☼ **LUNCH**   🌙 **DINNER**

Beef Liver and Eggs Scramble

Serves: 1

INGREDIENTS:
- 100g beef liver, sliced thinly
- 2 large eggs
- 1 tbsp butter or ghee
- Salt and pepper to taste
- Fresh parsley for garnish (optional)

STEPS:
In a skillet, melt the butter over medium heat.
Add the beef liver slices and cook until browned, about 3 minutes per side.
Crack the eggs into the skillet, season with salt and pepper, and scramble with the beef liver until the eggs are fully cooked.
Serve hot, garnished with parsley if desired.

Fact: Beef liver is one of the most nutrient-dense foods you can eat. It's rich in essential vitamins like B12, Vitamin A, and iron.

Bone Broth with Beef Slices

Serves: 1

INGREDIENTS:
- 2 cups bone broth
- 100g beef slices
- Salt to taste
- Green onions, chopped (optional)

STEPS:
Heat the bone broth in a pot over medium heat.
Once it starts to boil, add the beef slices and let them cook until tender.
Season with salt and serve hot, garnished with green onions if desired.

Fact: Bone broth is known for its gut-healing properties and is rich in collagen, which is beneficial for skin and joint health.

Grilled Chicken Thighs with Butter

Serves: 1

INGREDIENTS:

- 2 chicken thighs, bone-in and skin-on
- 1 tbsp butter
- Salt and pepper to taste
- Fresh lemon wedges (optional)

STEPS:

Preheat grill or grill pan over medium heat.

Season the chicken thighs with salt and pepper.

Place the chicken, skin-side down, on the grill. Cook for about 6-7 minutes per side or until fully cooked.

Serve hot with a dollop of butter on top and lemon wedges on the side.

Fact: Chicken thighs are a great source of healthy fats and are more flavorful than chicken breasts. They're also an excellent source of essential amino acids.

DAY 2

☀ **BREAKFAST**   ☼ **LUNCH**   ☾ **DINNER**

Pork Belly Slices and Scrambled Eggs

Serves: 1

INGREDIENTS:
- 3 slices of pork belly
- 2 large eggs
- 1 tbsp butter or ghee
- Salt and pepper to taste
- Fresh chives for garnish (optional)

STEPS:
In a skillet, cook the pork belly slices over medium heat until crispy and golden.
Remove the pork belly and drain on paper towels.
In the same skillet, melt the butter.
Crack the eggs into the skillet, season with salt and pepper, and scramble until fully cooked.
Serve hot with the pork belly slices, garnished with chives if desired.

Fact: Pork belly is rich in healthy fats that can help keep you full for longer. Plus, it's deliciously crispy when cooked right!

Lamb Chops with Bone Marrow Butter

Serves: 1

INGREDIENTS:
- 2 lamb chops
- 2 tbsp bone marrow butter
- Salt and pepper to taste
- Rosemary sprigs (optional)

STEPS:
Preheat grill or grill pan over medium heat.
Season the lamb chops with salt and pepper.
Grill the lamb chops for about 4-5 minutes per side or until your desired doneness.
Serve hot, topped with bone marrow butter and garnished with rosemary sprigs if desired.

Fact: Lamb is a great source of Vitamin B12, iron, and omega-3 fatty acids. It's also leaner than beef, offering a diverse meat option for those on the carnivore diet.

Grass-fed Steak with Garlic Butter

Serves: 1

INGREDIENTS:

- 1 grass-fed steak (around 200g)
- 2 tbsp garlic butter
- Salt and pepper to taste
- Fresh thyme for garnish (optional)

STEPS:

Allow the steak to come to room temperature for about 30 minutes.
Preheat grill or skillet over medium-high heat.
Season the steak with salt and pepper.
Cook the steak to your preferred level of doneness.
Serve hot with a dollop of garlic butter on top and garnished with fresh thyme if desired.

Fact: Grass-fed beef is richer in certain nutrients than grain-fed beef, including omega-3 fatty acids and Vitamin E.

DAY 3

☀ **BREAKFAST** ☼ **LUNCH** ☾ **DINNER**

Beef Sausages with Fried Eggs

Serves: 1

INGREDIENTS:
- 2 beef sausages
- 2 large eggs
- 1 tbsp butter or ghee
- Salt and pepper to taste

STEPS:
In a skillet, cook the beef sausages over medium heat until browned and fully cooked.
In the same skillet, melt the butter and fry the eggs to your liking.
Season the eggs with salt and pepper.
Serve hot with the beef sausages.

Fact: Beef sausages provide a good mix of protein and fats, making them a filling breakfast choice on the carnivore diet.

Chicken Wings with Hot Sauce

Serves: 1

INGREDIENTS:
- 6 chicken wings
- 2 tbsp hot sauce (make sure it's free from sugar and additives)
- Salt to taste

STEPS:
Preheat your oven to 425°F (220°C).
Season the chicken wings with salt.
Place them on a baking tray lined with parchment paper.
Bake for about 25-30 minutes or until golden and crispy.
Toss the baked wings in the hot sauce.
Serve hot.

Fact: Chicken wings are a great source of collagen due to the skin and connective tissues. This makes them beneficial for skin, hair, and joint health.

Salmon Filet with Lemon Butter

Serves: 1

INGREDIENTS:

- 1 salmon filet (around 150g)
- 1 tbsp lemon butter
- Salt and pepper to taste
- Lemon wedges for serving

STEPS:

Preheat a skillet over medium heat.
Season the salmon filet with salt and pepper.
Cook the salmon skin-side down for about 4 minutes, then flip and cook for another 2-3 minutes or
until done to your liking.
Serve hot with a dollop of lemon butter and lemon wedges on the side.

Fact: Salmon is a fatty fish that's rich in omega-3 fatty acids, which are known to support heart health, reduce inflammation, and improve brain function.

DAY 4

 BREAKFAST    LUNCH   ☾ DINNER

Beef and Egg Patty

Serves: 1

INGREDIENTS:
- 100g ground beef
- 1 large egg
- Salt and pepper to taste
- 1 tbsp butter or ghee

STEPS:
In a bowl, mix the ground beef, egg, salt, and pepper until well combined.
Shape the mixture into a patty.
In a skillet, melt the butter and cook the patty on medium heat until fully cooked, about 3-4 minutes each side.
Serve hot.

Fact: Combining beef with eggs not only enhances the protein content but also provides essential amino acids and a range of vitamins and minerals.

Pork Ribs

Serves: 1

INGREDIENTS:
- 3-4 pork ribs
- Salt and pepper to taste

STEPS:
Preheat the oven to 300°F (150°C).
Season the ribs with salt and pepper.
Place ribs on a baking sheet and bake for 2.5 to 3 hours, or until tender.
Serve hot.

Fact: Pork ribs are not only tasty but also rich in collagen, beneficial for maintaining healthy skin and joints.

Tuna Steaks with Olive Oil Drizzle

Serves: 1

INGREDIENTS:

- 1 tuna steak (about 150g)
- 2 tbsp olive oil
- Salt and pepper to taste
- Lemon wedges for serving

STEPS:

Preheat a skillet over medium-high heat.
Season the tuna steak with salt and pepper.
Sear the tuna steak for about 1-2 minutes on each side, depending on desired doneness.
Drizzle with olive oil and serve with lemon wedges.

Fact: Tuna is a rich source of omega-3 fatty acids, which can aid in reducing inflammation and supporting cardiovascular health.

DAY 5

BREAKFAST ☀ LUNCH ☾ DINNER

Beef Bacon and Boiled Eggs

Serves: 1

INGREDIENTS:
- 3 slices of beef bacon
- 2 large eggs

STEPS:
In a skillet, cook the beef bacon slices over medium heat until crispy.
In a pot, bring water to a boil. Gently add eggs and boil for 9-12 minutes, depending on desired consistency.
Peel the eggs and serve with the crispy beef bacon.

Fact: Beef bacon offers a smoky flavor similar to pork bacon but can be leaner and higher in protein.

Turkey Drumsticks

Serves: 1

INGREDIENTS:
- 1 turkey drumstick
- Salt and pepper to taste

STEPS:
Preheat the oven to 375°F (190°C).
Season the drumstick with salt and pepper.
Place it on a baking sheet and bake for about 40-50 minutes, or until fully cooked.
Serve hot.

Fact: Turkey is a lean source of protein and is rich in various vitamins and minerals, including niacin and selenium.

Sardines in Olive Oil

Serves: 1

INGREDIENTS:

- 1 can of sardines in olive oil
- Lemon wedges for serving

STEPS:

Open the can and plate the sardines.
Serve with lemon wedges.

Fact: Sardines are an excellent source of omega-3 fatty acids, calcium, and vitamin D, making them a nutrient powerhouse for those on a carnivore diet.

DAY 6

☀ BREAKFAST　　☼ LUNCH　　☾ DINNER

Ground Beef with Eggs

Serves: 1

INGREDIENTS:
- 100g ground beef
- 2 large eggs
- Salt and pepper to taste
- 1 tbsp butter or ghee

STEPS:
In a skillet, cook the ground beef until browned. Push to one side.
In the same skillet, melt butter and fry the eggs to your liking.
Season with salt and pepper.
Serve hot with the beef.

Fact: Ground beef is versatile and when paired with eggs, it makes a complete, nutrient-dense breakfast to start the day.

Chicken Breast with Herb Butter

Serves: 1

INGREDIENTS:
- 1 chicken breast
- 2 tbsp herb butter (a mixture of butter,
- chopped parsley, chives, and
- a pinch of salt)
- Salt and pepper to taste

STEPS:
Preheat a skillet over medium heat.
Season the chicken breast with salt and pepper.
Cook in the skillet for about 7-8 minutes on each side or until fully cooked.
Top with a dollop of herb butter and let it melt over the hot chicken breast.

Fact: Chicken breast is a lean protein that can be made delicious and moist with the addition of flavorful herb butter.

Trout with Clarified Butter

Serves: 1

INGREDIENTS:

- 1 trout fillet
- 2 tbsp clarified butter (ghee)
- Salt and pepper to taste
- Lemon wedges for serving

STEPS:

Preheat a skillet over medium-high heat.
Season the trout fillet with salt and pepper.
Cook the trout in the skillet for about 3-4 minutes on each side or until done to your liking.
Drizzle with clarified butter and serve with lemon wedges.

Fact: Trout, like other fatty fish, is a great source of omega-3 fatty acids and pairs wonderfully with the rich taste of clarified butter.

DAY 7

☀ **BREAKFAST**   ☼ **LUNCH**   ☾ **DINNER**

Lamb Sausages with Poached Eggs

Serves: 1

INGREDIENTS:
- 2 lamb sausages
- 2 large eggs
- 1 tbsp vinegar
- Salt to taste

STEPS:
In a skillet, cook the lamb sausages over medium heat until browned and cooked through.
In a pot, bring water to a light simmer. Add vinegar.
Crack one egg into a bowl, then gently slide it into the simmering water. Repeat with the other egg.
Poach the eggs for about 4 minutes or until whites are set but yolks remain runny.
Using a slotted spoon, transfer eggs to a plate. Season with salt.
Serve poached eggs alongside the lamb sausages.

Fact: Lamb sausages provide a tasty variation from the regular pork or beef sausages and are rich in various nutrients like Vitamin B12.

Bone-in Ribeye Steak

Serves: 1

INGREDIENTS:
- 1 bone-in ribeye steak (around 250g)
- Salt and pepper to taste
- 2 tbsp butter or ghee

STEPS:
Allow the steak to come to room temperature for about 30 minutes.
Preheat a skillet over medium-high heat.
Season the steak generously with salt and pepper.
Melt butter in the skillet and add the steak.
Cook to your preferred level of doneness, basting with butter occasionally.
Let the steak rest for 5 minutes before serving.

Fact: Bone-in steaks tend to be juicier and more flavorful as the bone imparts a deeper taste during the cooking process.

Grilled Shrimp with Lime Butter

Serves: 1

INGREDIENTS:

- 8-10 large shrimps, peeled and deveined
- 2 tbsp lime butter (a mixture of butter, lime zest, and a pinch of salt)
- Salt and pepper to taste

STEPS:

Preheat a grill or grill pan over medium-high heat.
Season the shrimps with salt and pepper.
Grill the shrimps for about 1-2 minutes on each side or until they turn pink and are cooked through.
Serve the shrimps with a dollop of lime butter on top.

Fact: Shrimps are low in fat and calories, yet high in protein. They also contain essential antioxidants and omega-3 fatty acids.

WHY WEEK 1 IS CRUCIAL

"Remember when you tried to learn the guitar, and those first few chords felt alien to your fingers? But soon, they became second nature. That's Week 1 for you in this carnivore journey!"

Diving into a new diet isn't just about the food. It's about rewriting your culinary script, unlearning old habits, and embracing a whole new rhythm. This pivotal first week serves as your introduction to the carnivore world, where you set the tone for the following weeks. It's the foundation, the base camp if you will, from which you'll ascend to greater dietary heights. Like any significant change, there will be moments of doubt, maybe even resistance. But remember, it's in these initial phases that you're recalibrating your body and mind. Each meal is a step toward reconditioning not just your palate but your entire metabolic system. Think of it as updating the software on your phone; it might be a bit glitchy at first, but once it settles, you're operating on a whole new level.

Adjusting Your Palate

"It's like having worn sunglasses all day and then suddenly taking them off in the evening. Everything seems brighter, more vivid. That's your palate without the overwhelming influence of sugars and processed foods."

Throughout our lives, our taste buds have been drowned in a cacophony of flavors - many artificial, some overwhelmingly strong. As you embark on this carnivore journey, you're giving your palate a detox of sorts. At first, everything might taste 'plain' or 'bland'. But that's just the noise of past diets fading away. Soon, you'll start discerning subtle flavors in meats you never noticed before. A steak will no longer be just salty; you might pick up hints of nuttiness, sweetness, or even earthiness, depending on the cut and how it's prepared. This week is your sensory reset button. It's about rediscovering the authentic flavors that nature intended and letting your taste buds truly savor them without distractions.

Getting Over the Carb Hump

"Imagine your body's been running on regular AA batteries, and suddenly you're switching to high-powered lithium cells. There's going to be an adjustment period!"

Carbohydrates, especially sugars, have been the quick-and-easy fuel for our bodies for a long time. As you reduce your carb intake during this first week, you might experience what many refer to as the 'low-carb flu'. This is your body's transition from burning carbs for energy to burning fats. It's like a car getting used to a different fuel type. You might feel sluggish, perhaps a tad irritable, or even experience mild headaches. But fear not! This is temporary. Your body is an adaptable machine. Once it recognizes fat as its primary fuel source, you'll start feeling more energetic, your mind might seem sharper, and those afternoon energy slumps? A thing of the past. This week, patience is your ally. Drink plenty of water, ensure you're getting enough electrolytes, and trust in your body's remarkable ability to adjust.

Meat: Your New BFF

"Ever had that feeling when you rewatch a movie and notice details you never did the first time? That's you with meat this week. You're about to discover layers and nuances you never knew existed!"

In the carnivore diet, meat isn't just a component of your meal; it's the star of the show. This week, you're going beyond just grilling a steak or frying up some bacon. You're delving deep into the world of meats. From understanding different cuts and their flavors to exploring preparation techniques that bring out the best in them, you're on a carnivorous culinary adventure. It's also about understanding the source of your meat. Grass-fed, grain-fed, aged - these aren't just labels; they tell a story of the meat you're consuming. By the end of this week, you won't just be eating meat; you'll be experiencing it. You'll be forming a bond with your food, understanding its origins, and savoring every bite with newfound appreciation.

WEEK 2

Nourish and Flourish - Embracing the Nutrient Beats

The Importance of Variety in Your Meaty Menu

"You know how a playlist with just one song on repeat can get boring, no matter how much you love the track? The same goes for your diet. It's time to shuffle and explore new meaty tunes!"

If Week 1 was about getting your foot in the door, Week 2 is about dancing through the carnivore banquet hall! While it might seem that a carnivore diet restricts you to a monotonous menu, it's quite the opposite. Our planet offers a plethora of meats, each with its own nutrient profile, taste, and texture. This week, it's all about embracing that diversity and ensuring your body is not just adapting but thriving on this new lifestyle.

Balancing Your Meat Portfolio

"Think of your diet as an investment portfolio. You wouldn't put all your money in one stock, would you? Similarly, diversifying your meat intake is key to reaping maximum nutritional dividends!"

From beef, chicken, and pork to more exotic choices like lamb, bison, and even game meats - the world of carnivory is vast and varied. Each meat type offers a unique set of nutrients. For instance, while beef is an excellent source of iron and B-vitamins, fish provides essential omega-3 fatty acids. By rotating these meats, you're not just treating your palate to a gourmet experience but also ensuring a balanced intake of vitamins, minerals, and other essential nutrients.

Beyond Muscle Meat: Offal Offerings

"Ever ignored the bonus tracks on an album, only to discover later they're hidden gems? That's offal for you - the often-overlooked bonus tracks of the carnivore world!"

While steaks and chicken breasts are crowd-pleasers, organ meats or offals like liver, kidney, and heart are nutritional powerhouses. They're densely packed with nutrients, often more so than muscle meats. For example, liver is nature's multivitamin, teeming with Vitamin A, folic acid, and several B-vitamins. This week, as you delve deeper into your meaty menu, don't sidestep these. They might be an acquired taste for some, but with the right recipes (which we'll explore this week!), you might just find a new favorite.

Seafood: The Ocean's Bounty

"Diving into the carnivore diet without exploring seafood is like visiting a theme park and skipping half the rides. You're missing out on a world of adventure!"

While terrestrial meats hold a prime spot in the carnivore diet, let's not forget the treasures the oceans and rivers bestow upon us. Fish, crustaceans, mollusks - they're not just delicious but are brimming with nutrients like iodine, selenium, and the aforementioned omega-3s. Incorporating a variety of seafood ensures you're getting a spectrum of nutrients and also breaks the monotony, adding a splash of marine flavors to your plate.

DAY 8

☀ BREAKFAST   ☼ LUNCH   ☾ DINNER

Venison Patties with Eggs

Serves: 1

INGREDIENTS:
- 2 venison patties
- 2 large eggs
- 1 tbsp butter or ghee
- Salt and pepper to taste

STEPS:
In a skillet, cook the venison patties on medium heat until fully cooked, flipping once.
Push the patties to one side and melt butter in the skillet.
Crack the eggs into the skillet and fry to your desired consistency.
Season with salt and pepper and serve alongside the patties.

Fact: Venison is low in fat and high in protein. It also contains iron and essential B vitamins.

Swordfish with Garlic Butter

Serves: 1

INGREDIENTS:
- 1 swordfish steak
- 2 tbsp garlic butter (butter mixed with minced garlic)
- Salt and pepper to taste
- Lemon wedges for serving

STEPS:
Season the swordfish steak with salt and pepper.
In a skillet over medium heat, melt the garlic butter.
Add the swordfish and cook until done to your liking.
Serve hot with lemon wedges.

Fact: Swordfish is a meaty fish rich in omega-3 fatty acids and pairs wonderfully with the aromatic garlic butter.

Duck Breast with Orange Reduction

Serves: 1

INGREDIENTS:

- 1 duck breast
- Juice of 1 orange
- Salt and pepper to taste

STEPS:

Score the skin of the duck breast.
Season both sides with salt and pepper.
Start cooking the duck breast skin-side down on a cold skillet. Turn the heat to medium and cook until the skin is crispy.
Flip and cook the other side.
Remove the duck and set aside. Drain the excess fat.
Pour the orange juice into the skillet and let it reduce by half.
Slice the duck breast and serve with the orange reduction.

Fact: Duck is a rich source of protein and provides a unique taste. The orange reduction complements the rich flavor of the duck.

DAY 9

☀ BREAKFAST ☀ LUNCH ☾ DINNER

Bone Marrow with Toasted Liver Pâté

Serves: 1

INGREDIENTS:
- 2 bone marrow pieces
- 2 slices of liver pâté
- Toast for serving
- Salt to taste

STEPS:
Preheat the oven to 425°F (220°C).
Place bone marrow pieces in an ovenproof dish, seasoned side up.
Roast for about 15-20 minutes or until marrow is soft and bubbly.
Toast slices of liver pâté until slightly crispy.
Spread the bone marrow onto the toasted pâté slices and season with salt.

Fact: Bone marrow is a rich source of fats and nutrients. When paired with liver pâté, it becomes a superfood-rich breakfast.

Beef Brisket

Serves: 1

INGREDIENTS:
- 200g beef brisket
- Salt and pepper to taste

STEPS:
Preheat the oven to 300°F (150°C).
Season the brisket with salt and pepper.
Place in an ovenproof dish and cover with aluminum foil.
Cook for 3-4 hours or until tender.
Slice and serve.

Fact: Beef brisket is a flavorful cut of meat that becomes tender and juicy when cooked slowly.

Lobster Tail with Drawn Butter

Serves: 1

INGREDIENTS:

- 1 lobster tail
- 2 tbsp drawn butter
- Lemon wedges for serving

STEPS:

Preheat the grill or oven to 400°F (205°C).
Cut the top shell of the lobster tail lengthwise and pull the meat upwards, letting it sit on top of the shell.
Grill or bake for about 8-10 minutes or until the lobster meat is opaque.
Serve with drawn butter and lemon wedges.

Fact: Lobster is not only a delicacy but also a good source of zinc, selenium, and vitamin B12.

DAY 10

☀ BREAKFAST ☀ LUNCH ☾ DINNER

Ground Bison and Eggs Scramble

Serves: 1

INGREDIENTS:
- 100g ground bison
- 2 large eggs
- 1 tbsp butter or ghee
- Salt and pepper to taste

STEPS:
In a skillet, cook the ground bison until browned.
Push the bison to one side and melt the butter in the skillet.
Pour the beaten eggs into the skillet and scramble.
Mix with the bison, season with salt and pepper, and serve.

Fact: Bison is leaner than beef and has a richer, sweeter flavor. It is also a good source of protein and iron.

Mackerel with Olive Oil

Serves: 1

INGREDIENTS:
- 1 mackerel fillet
- 2 tbsp olive oil
- Salt and lemon zest to taste

STEPS:
Season the mackerel fillet with salt and lemon zest.
In a skillet over medium heat, add the olive oil.
Once hot, add the mackerel, skin side down, and cook until crispy.
Flip and cook the other side until done.
Serve drizzled with the remaining olive oil.

Fact: Mackerel is an oily fish that's high in omega-3 fatty acids. It's great for heart health and pairs beautifully with the richness of olive oil.

Roast Chicken Leg Quarter

Serves: 1

INGREDIENTS:

- 1 chicken leg quarter
- Salt, pepper, and herbs to taste
- (e.g., rosemary, thyme)

STEPS:

Preheat the oven to 375°F (190°C).
Season the chicken with salt, pepper, and herbs.
Place in an ovenproof dish and roast for about 40-45 minutes or until fully cooked.
Serve hot.

Fact: Chicken is a lean source of protein. The leg quarter is juicier and has a richer flavor compared to the breast.

DAY 11

☀ BREAKFAST ☼ LUNCH ☾ DINNER

Pork Sausage with Fried Eggs

Serves: 1

INGREDIENTS:
- 2 pork sausages
- 2 large eggs
- 1 tbsp butter or ghee
- Salt and pepper to taste

STEPS:
Cook the pork sausages in a skillet over medium heat until fully cooked.
Push the sausages to one side and melt the butter in the skillet.
Crack the eggs into the skillet and fry to your desired consistency.
Season with salt and pepper and serve with the sausages.

Fact: Pork sausages are flavorful and provide a good amount of protein. When paired with eggs, they make a satisfying and energy-boosting breakfast.

Roast Leg of Lamb

Serves: 1

INGREDIENTS:

- 200g leg of lamb slice
- 2 cloves garlic, minced
- Rosemary, thyme, salt, and pepper

STEPS:

Preheat the oven to 325°F (165°C).

Rub the lamb with garlic, rosemary, thyme, salt, and pepper.

Place in an ovenproof dish and roast for about 25-30 minutes or until done to your liking.

Let it rest for a few minutes, then slice and serve.

Fact: Lamb is tender and flavorful, and it's a good source of protein, vitamins, and minerals.

Beef Meatballs

Serves: 1

INGREDIENTS:

- 5-6 beef meatballs (pre-made or homemade)
- 1 tbsp olive oil
- Salt and herbs to taste
- (e.g., basil, oregano)

STEPS:

In a skillet over medium heat, add the olive oil.

Once hot, add the meatballs and cook until browned and fully cooked inside.

Season with salt and herbs, and serve.

Fact: Beef meatballs are versatile and can be seasoned in numerous ways. They are a great source of protein and iron.

DAY 12

☀️ **BREAKFAST**   ☀ **LUNCH**   🌙 **DINNER**

Ground Turkey and Egg Patty

Serves: 1

INGREDIENTS:

- 100g ground turkey
- 1 large egg
- 1 tbsp butter or ghee
- Salt, pepper, and herbs to taste

STEPS:

In a bowl, mix the ground turkey, egg, salt, pepper, and herbs.
Shape into a patty.
In a skillet, melt the butter over medium heat.
Add the patty and cook until browned on both sides and fully cooked inside.
Serve hot.

Fact: Ground turkey is leaner than beef and is a good source of essential nutrients like niacin and vitamin B6.

Salmon Roe with Cream Cheese

Serves: 1

INGREDIENTS:

- 2 tbsp salmon roe
- 2 tbsp cream cheese
- Crackers or toast for serving

STEPS:

Spread cream cheese on crackers or toast.
Top with salmon roe.
Serve immediately.

Fact: Salmon roe is rich in omega-3 fatty acids, which are beneficial for heart and brain health. The combination of creamy cheese and the burst of flavor from the roe is simply delightful.

Beef Tenderloin with Herb Butter

Serves: 1

INGREDIENTS:

- 1 beef tenderloin steak
- 2 tbsp herb butter (butter mixed with minced garlic, parsley, and a pinch of salt)
- Salt and pepper to taste

STEPS:

Season the steak with salt and pepper.
In a skillet over medium heat, melt half of the herb butter.
Add the steak and cook until done to your liking, adding more herb butter as needed.
Serve with the remaining herb butter on top.

Fact: Beef tenderloin is one of the most tender cuts of beef. The herb butter enhances its natural flavors.

DAY 13

☀ **BREAKFAST**　　☼ **LUNCH**　　☾ **DINNER**

Beef Jerky with Boiled Eggs

Serves: 1

INGREDIENTS:
- 3-4 pieces of beef jerky
- 2 large eggs

STEPS:
Boil the eggs to your desired consistency.
Peel and serve with beef jerky on the side.

Fact: Beef jerky is a high-protein snack that is cured and dried. Paired with eggs, it provides a protein-packed start to your day.

Smoked Pork Shoulder

Serves: 1

INGREDIENTS:
- 200g smoked pork shoulder slice
- 1 tbsp BBQ sauce (optional)

STEPS:
Warm the pork shoulder in an oven or skillet.
Slice and serve with BBQ sauce if desired.

Fact: Smoked pork shoulder is tender and flavorful due to the slow smoking process. It's a good source of protein and essential nutrients.

Grilled Calamari with Olive Oil

Serves: 1

INGREDIENTS:

- 5-6 calamari rings or tubes
- 2 tbsp olive oil
- Salt, pepper, and lemon zest to taste

STEPS:

Season the calamari with salt, pepper, and lemon zest.
Preheat a grill or grill pan over medium-high heat.
Brush the calamari with olive oil and grill for 1-2 minutes on each side or until they turn opaque.
Serve with a drizzle of olive oil.

Fact: Calamari is low in calories but high in protein. It's also a good source of selenium and vitamin B12.

DAY 14

☀ BREAKFAST ☀ LUNCH ☾ DINNER

Chorizo with Scrambled Eggs

Serves: 1

INGREDIENTS:
- 100g chorizo, sliced or crumbled
- 2 large eggs, beaten
- 1 tbsp butter or ghee
- Salt and pepper to taste
- Fresh herbs for garnish (optional)

STEPS:
In a skillet, cook the chorizo until slightly crispy and its oils are released.

Push the chorizo to one side and melt butter in the skillet.

Pour the beaten eggs into the skillet and gently scramble, mixing with the chorizo.

Season with salt and pepper and serve garnished with fresh herbs if desired.

Fact: Chorizo, a spicy sausage, adds a punch of flavor to dishes. When combined with eggs, it provides a spicy, savory start to the day.

Venison Roast

Serves: 1

INGREDIENTS:
- 200g venison roast
- 1 tbsp olive oil
- Salt, pepper, and rosemary to taste

STEPS:
Preheat the oven to 325°F (165°C).

Season the venison with salt, pepper, and rosemary.

In a skillet, heat the olive oil on high heat. Sear the venison on all sides until browned.

Transfer the venison to an ovenproof dish and roast for about 20-25 minutes or until cooked to your desired doneness.

Let it rest for a few minutes, then slice and serve.

Fact: Venison is leaner than many other meats and is high in protein. It offers a unique flavor, enhanced by the aromatic rosemary.

Chicken Livers with Butter

Serves: 1

INGREDIENTS:

- 150g chicken livers, cleaned and
- trimmed
- 2 tbsp butter
- 1 small onion, finely chopped
- 2 cloves garlic, minced
- Salt and pepper to taste
- Fresh parsley, chopped (for garnish)

STEPS:

In a skillet, melt 1 tbsp of butter over medium heat.
Add the onion and garlic, and sauté until translucent.
Push the onion and garlic to the side and add the remaining butter.
Increase the heat to medium-high and add the chicken livers.
Sauté them until they are browned
on the outside but still slightly pink in the middle.
Season with salt and pepper.
Serve hot, garnished with fresh parsley.

Fact: Chicken livers are incredibly nutrient-dense. They're a great source of iron, vitamin A, and B vitamins, especially folate and B12.

WEEK 2: NOURISH AND FLOURISH – EMBRACING THE NUTRIENT BEATS

End of Week Reflection

Physical Fitness Tip: Introducing Strength Training
Have you ever tried lifting weights? No, I'm not suggesting you go full Schwarzenegger, but a little strength training goes a long way. Think of strength training like adding a shiny new sports car engine to your already fantastic car body. It revs up the metabolism, and trust me, there's nothing quite as satisfying as feeling those muscles you never knew existed!
Why is strength training beneficial, especially on a carnivore diet? Well, the proteins and nutrients you're ingesting are perfect for muscle repair and growth. By introducing light weights or even bodyweight exercises into your routine, you'll be harnessing the full potential of this diet. Start with simple exercises like squats, push-ups, or lunges. Always remember, it's not about how much weight you lift, but how consistently you do it!

Mental Shifts: Gaining Mental Clarity and Focus
Ever heard of the term 'brain fog'? It's that feeling where you're not quite here nor there. It's like trying to drive in heavy fog with just your parking lights on. Not ideal, right? Now, imagine a windscreen wiper for your brain. That's Week 2 for you! Many people on the carnivore diet report clearer thinking and a sharper focus.
Why does this happen? Some believe it's due to reduced sugar intake leading to steadier blood sugar levels. Sugar spikes can lead to rapid energy drops, causing that foggy feeling. By maintaining a steady intake of protein-rich foods, you're giving your brain a consistent energy source, letting it function optimally. It's like upgrading from regular fuel to premium for your car!

Health Checkpoint: Observing Improved Digestion and Energy Levels
Let's talk about that glorious machine that is our digestive system. Imagine it as a conveyor belt at the airport. When it's overloaded or jammed with bags (or in our case, different foods), it struggles. But when things are smooth and streamlined, it's a sight to behold!
On a carnivore diet, especially in Week 2, many folks notice smoother digestion. This might be because the diet is simpler, and your body doesn't have to work overtime to process various food types. Protein and fat from meat can be easier for some people to digest, leading to less bloating and discomfort. And then there's energy. On this diet, you're switching your primary energy source from carbs to fats, which burn longer and steadier. It's like having a slow-burning candle versus a quick flash of light. You might just find yourself with a pep in your step and ready to take on the wo

WEEK 3

Renew and Rejoice - The Refreshing Remix

The Balance Between Fats and Proteins

Imagine, if you will, a well-choreographed dance. Two dancers, moving with grace and precision, each complementing the other's moves, never overshadowing, always in harmony. In the dance of our diet, these two pivotal dancers are fats and proteins. And Week 3 is all about understanding and appreciating their elegant waltz.

Fats: The Unsung Hero

Picture fats as the quiet but strong lead dancer, guiding the dance and providing the energy. Fats have often been villainized, but in a carnivore diet, they're the stars! They're the primary source of energy, giving us that slow-burning fuel we talked about in Week 2. It's the kind of sustained energy that ensures you don't crash midday, yearning for a nap. Plus, fats help in the absorption of certain vital vitamins like A, D, E, and K. It's like the backstage crew in a play, ensuring the star (that's you!) shines bright.

Proteins: The Building Blocks

Now, enter proteins - the agile, nimble dancer, ensuring growth and repair. Every cell in our body contains protein. Think of them as the bricks and mortar holding our body together. They help repair tissues, make enzymes and hormones, and play a crucial role in bones, muscles, cartilage, skin, and blood health. On this diet, proteins ensure you're not just running smoothly, but you're also building and repairing as you go. It's like having a team of builders and mechanics working around the clock just for you.

Striking the Balance

Getting the ratio of fats to proteins right is the crux of Week 3. Too much of one can overshadow the other, throwing our dance out of rhythm. Aim for a mix that provides satiety, energy, and all the building blocks your body needs. Remember, it's not a one-size-fits-all approach. What works for Fred Astaire might not work for Ginger Rogers! Listen to your body, adjust as needed, and relish the harmony.

This week, as you delve deeper into the carnivore diet, envision yourself as the choreographer of this beautiful dance. You hold the power to balance, tweak, and perfect the rhythm. So, lace up your dancing shoes, let fats and proteins take the lead, and dance your way to renewed health and vitality!

DAY 15

☀ **BREAKFAST** ☼ **LUNCH** ☾ **DINNER**

Pork Loin and Eggs

Serves: 1

INGREDIENTS:

- 100g pork loin, thinly sliced
- 2 eggs, any style
- 1 tbsp butter or ghee
- Salt and pepper to taste

STEPS:

In a skillet, melt butter and cook pork loin slices until slightly golden. Push the pork loin to one side and cook eggs as preferred. Season and serve.

Fact: Pork loin is a lean cut and can be a great source of protein to kickstart your day.

Slow-Cooked Beef Stew

Serves: 1

INGREDIENTS:

- 150g beef chunks
- 1 cup beef broth
- 1 bay leaf
- Salt and pepper to taste

STEPS:

In a slow cooker, combine beef, broth, bay leaf, salt, and pepper. Cook on low for 6-8 hours until beef is tender. Serve hot.

Fact: Slow cooking beef breaks down its fibers, making it tender and easier to digest.

Baked Cod with Lemon Butter

Serves: 1

INGREDIENTS:

- 150g cod fillet
- 2 tbsp butter
- 1 lemon wedge
- Salt and pepper to taste

STEPS:

Preheat oven to 350°F (175°C).
Season cod with salt and pepper and place in a baking dish.
Dot with butter and bake for 20 minutes or until cooked through.
Squeeze lemon over cod and serve.

Fact: Cod is a low-fat fish that's rich in vitamin B12 and iodine.

DAY 16

☀ BREAKFAST ☀ LUNCH ☾ DINNER

Ground Lamb with Poached Eggs

Serves: 1

INGREDIENTS:

- 100g ground lamb
- 2 eggs
- Salt and pepper to taste

STEPS:

In a skillet, cook ground lamb until browned. Season with salt and pepper.
In a separate pot, poach eggs to desired consistency.
Serve lamb topped with poached eggs.

Fact: Lamb is rich in essential amino acids and minerals like iron and zinc

Grilled Herring with Olive Oil

Serves: 1

INGREDIENTS:

- 1 herring fillet
- 2 tbsp olive oil
- Salt and pepper to taste

STEPS:

Season herring with salt and pepper.
Grill on each side for about 3 minutes.
Drizzle with olive oil and serve.

Fact: Herring is high in omega-3 fatty acids, which are great for heart health.

Beef Short Ribs

Serves: 1

INGREDIENTS:

- 150g beef short ribs
- 1 cup beef broth
- Salt and pepper to taste

STEPS:

In a pot, combine short ribs, broth, salt, and pepper.
Simmer until meat is tender and falling off the bone, about 2-3 hours.
Serve hot.

Fact: Short ribs, being a fatty cut, provide both protein and essential fats.

DAY 17

☀ BREAKFAST ☼ LUNCH ☾ DINNER

Beef Tongue Slices with Eggs

Serves: 1

INGREDIENTS:
- 3 slices of cooked beef tongue
- 2 eggs, any style
- 1 tbsp butter or ghee
- Salt and pepper to taste

STEPS:
In a pot, combine short ribs, broth, salt, and pepper.
Simmer until meat is tender and falling off the bone, about 2-3 hours.
Serve hot.

Fact: Beef tongue is a nutritional powerhouse, rich in fatty acids, vitamin B12, and other essential nutrients.

Rabbit Stew

Serves: 1

INGREDIENTS:
- 150g rabbit meat, chopped
- 1 cup chicken broth
- 1 bay leaf
- Salt and pepper to taste

STEPS:
Combine rabbit meat, broth, bay leaf, salt, and pepper in a pot.
Simmer until meat is tender, about 1-2 hours.
Serve hot.

Fact: Rabbit meat is lean and packed with high-quality proteins.

Trout Almandine with Butter

Serves: 1

INGREDIENTS:

- 1 trout fillet
- 2 tbsp butter
- A handful of sliced almonds
- Lemon wedge
- Salt and pepper to taste

STEPS:

Season trout with salt and pepper.
In a skillet, melt butter and place trout skin-side down.
Cook until skin is crispy, then flip and add almonds.
Squeeze lemon over trout before serving.

Fact: Trout provides omega-3 fatty acids and pairs exceptionally well with crunchy almonds.

DAY 18

☀ BREAKFAST   ☼ LUNCH   ☾ DINNER

Prosciutto with Fried Eggs

Serves: 1

INGREDIENTS:
- 3 slices of prosciutto
- 2 eggs
- 1 tbsp olive oil
- Salt and pepper to taste

STEPS:
Lay out prosciutto slices on a plate.
In a skillet, heat olive oil and fry eggs to your liking.
Place eggs over prosciutto. Season and serve.

Fact: Prosciutto is a source of vitamin B1 which helps convert food into energy.

Grilled Octopus with Lemon Olive Oil

Serves: 1

INGREDIENTS:
- 100g octopus tentacles, pre-cooked
- 2 tbsp olive oil
- Lemon zest and juice
- Salt and pepper to taste

STEPS:
Combine olive oil, lemon zest, and juice.
Grill octopus until slightly charred.
Drizzle with lemon olive oil before serving.

Fact: Octopus is an excellent source of taurine, an amino sulfonic acid essential for cardiovascular function.

Osso Buco

Serves: 1

INGREDIENTS:

- 1 veal shank
- 1 cup beef broth
- 1 bay leaf
- Salt and pepper to taste

STEPS:

Season veal shank with salt and pepper.
Place in a pot with broth and bay leaf.
Simmer until meat is tender and falling off the bone, about 2-3 hours.
Serve hot.

Fact: Osso Buco, traditionally made from veal shanks, contains marrow which is rich in nutrients.

DAY 19

☀ BREAKFAST　　☀ LUNCH　　☾ DINNER

Beef Pastrami and Eggs

Serves: 1

INGREDIENTS:
- 3 slices beef pastrami
- 2 eggs
- 1 tbsp butter or ghee
- Salt and pepper to taste

STEPS:
In a skillet, warm up beef pastrami.
Push to one side and cook eggs as preferred.
Season and serve.

Fact: Pastrami undergoes a lengthy curing process which amplifies its flavor and nutrient content.

Bison Steak

Serves: 1

INGREDIENTS:
- 150g bison steak
- 1 tbsp butter or ghee
- Salt and pepper to taste

STEPS:
Season bison steak.
In a hot skillet, sear steak in butter to your desired doneness.
Let rest for a few minutes, then serve.

Fact: Bison is leaner than beef but offers a similar nutrient profile with a slightly sweeter taste.

Oysters with Lemon Juice

Serves: 1

INGREDIENTS:

- 6 fresh oysters
- Lemon wedge
- Salt to taste

STEPS:

Shuck oysters and place on ice.
Squeeze lemon over them and season lightly with salt.
Serve immediately.

Fact: Oysters are a powerful source of zinc, essential for immune function and DNA synthesis.

DAY 20

☀ BREAKFAST　　☼ LUNCH　　☾ DINNER

Ground Chicken and Egg Patty

Serves: 1

INGREDIENTS:
- 100g ground chicken
- 1 egg
- 1 tbsp butter or ghee
- Salt and pepper to taste

STEPS:
In a bowl, mix ground chicken and egg.
Shape the mixture into a patty.
In a skillet, melt butter and cook the patty until golden brown on both sides.
Season and serve.

Fact: Chicken is a great source of niacin, a B-vitamin crucial for energy metabolism.

Sardines with Garlic Butter

Serves: 1

INGREDIENTS:
- 4-5 sardines, fresh or canned in olive oil
- 2 tbsp butter
- 2 garlic cloves, minced
- Lemon wedge
- Salt to taste

STEPS:
If using fresh sardines, clean and gut them.
In a skillet, melt butter and sauté garlic until fragrant.
Add sardines and cook until golden.
Squeeze lemon over them, season with salt, and serve.

Fact: Sardines are an excellent source of omega-3 fatty acids, which have been linked to numerous health benefits.

Pork Tenderloin

Serves: 1

INGREDIENTS:

- 150g pork tenderloin
- 1 tbsp olive oil
- Salt and pepper to taste

STEPS:

Season pork tenderloin with salt and pepper.
In a skillet, heat olive oil and sear pork on all sides.
Finish in the oven at 375°F (190°C) for about 12-15 minutes or until cooked through.
Let rest for a few minutes before slicing and serving.

Fact: Pork tenderloin is a lean cut of meat that's rich in thiamine, a B-vitamin important for nerve function.

DAY 21

☀ BREAKFAST ☀ LUNCH ☾ DINNER

Beef Salami with Scrambled Eggs

Serves: 1

INGREDIENTS:
- 3 slices beef salami
- 2 eggs
- 1 tbsp butter or ghee
- Salt and pepper to taste

STEPS:
In a skillet, warm up beef salami.
Push them to one side and scramble the eggs in butter.
Season and serve together.

Fact: Salami is often fermented, which can introduce beneficial bacteria to your gut.

Canned Tuna in Olive Oil

Serves: 1

INGREDIENTS:
- 1 can of tuna in olive oil
- Salt and pepper to taste
- Lemon wedge

STEPS:
Drain excess olive oil from the tuna.
Season with salt and pepper.
Squeeze lemon over the tuna and serve.

Fact: Tuna is an excellent source of lean protein and selenium, a mineral that acts as a powerful antioxidant.

Roast Duck Leg

Serves: 1

INGREDIENTS:
- 1 duck leg
- Salt and pepper to taste

STEPS:
Preheat the oven to 375°F (190°C).
Season duck leg with salt and pepper.
Roast in the oven for about 45 minutes or until skin is crispy and meat is cooked through.
Serve hot.

Fact: Duck is rich in monounsaturated fats, which can be heart-healthy when consumed in moderation.

WEEK 3: END OF WEEK REFLECTION- RENEW AND REJOICE - THE REFRESHING REMIX

Physical Fitness Tip: Cardio Sessions for Heart Health

Huffing and Puffing to the Beat of Your Heart

If you were a drum, your heart would be the rhythm. Cardio sessions are like jamming sessions for your internal drum. As you adapt to the carnivore diet, you're fueling your body with robust energy sources. It's like you've been practicing the guitar for ages, and suddenly someone hands you an electric guitar. Amp up your exercise game with some heart-pumping, toe-tapping cardio. Whether you groove to the Zumba beats, pound the pavements with a morning run, or glide through water with a swim - your heart benefits. Cardio not only keeps your heart in top shape but also complements the fats and proteins by ensuring they're efficiently burned for energy. Remember, even a brisk 30-minute walk can set the rhythm right.

Mental Shifts: Feeling More Connected and Present

Harnessing the Inner Zen

You ever tried tuning an old radio, turning the dial ever so slightly, trying to find that clear frequency? This week, with a balanced intake of fats and proteins, you might just find your mind doing something similar - tuning in clearer, eliminating the static. Being on the carnivore diet might be making you feel more connected, not just to yourself but also to your surroundings. Imagine walking in a garden and noticing details you previously overlooked: the dew on a leaf, the pattern on a butterfly's wing, or the distant sound of a bird's song. This newfound presence can be deeply enriching. Embrace it. It's like you've been handed a pair of high-definition glasses for life!

Health Checkpoint: Noticing Changes in Skin Health and Sleep Patterns

Sleeping Like a Baby and Glowing Like the Morning Sun

Your skin is like a billboard, advertising the state of your inner health. This week, don't be surprised if someone squints and says, "Is that a glow, or are you secretly a vampire?" Thanks to the wholesome nutrients, your skin might just be thanking you by looking clearer, feeling smoother, and exuding a natural shine. As for sleep, it's possibly deeper and more restorative. With fats slowly releasing energy, you're unlikely to wake up in the middle of the night with hunger pangs or sugar crashes. Think of it as being serenaded to sleep by a lullaby, ensuring you wake up feeling like you've been wrapped in a cloud. Sweet dreams and radiant mornings are the way forward

WEEK 4

Celebrate and Cultivate - The Encore of Excellence

The Culmination of Your Carnivore Journey

The Final Crescendo in a Symphony of Meaty Melodies

By now, you're not just someone who's eaten a steak or two; you've ventured through a carnivorous odyssey. It's like you've been listening to a concert, and we're finally at the heart-thumping finale. This week isn't just about wrapping things up; it's about recognizing the shifts, relishing the rewards, and preparing for the road ahead.

The Evolution: Just as a caterpillar transforms into a butterfly, your journey over these past weeks has been transformative. The initial curiosity, the adaptation, and now, the deepening understanding of this diet. Remember the hesitant first bite? Now you're here, a culinary maestro of meats!

Balancing the Act: It's not just about gobbling up proteins and fats; it's about the art of balance. This week, think of fine-tuning that balance. Imagine being a juggler, ensuring each element - from the juicy steaks to the fatty fish - gets its moment in the spotlight, maintaining that carnivore equilibrium.

Embracing the New Normal: Just as an artist prepares for an encore, this isn't the end but rather a new beginning. It's a commitment to continually refine and explore. As you move forward, each day can be a fresh page, where you draw upon your experiences and paint a vibrant carnivore canvas.

So, as we dive into the final week, let's not just finish the journey; let's celebrate each bite, each insight, and most importantly, the newfound understanding of your body. Here's to the encore of excellence! Cheers!

DAY 22

☀ **BREAKFAST** ☼ **LUNCH** ☾ **DINNER**

Elk Patties with Eggs

Serves: 1

INGREDIENTS:
- 100g ground elk
- 1 egg
- 1 tbsp butter or ghee
- Salt and pepper to taste

STEPS:
Shape the ground elk into a patty.
In a skillet, melt butter and cook the patty until it's browned on both sides.
Fry the egg in the same pan.
Season both patty and egg, then serve.

Fact: Elk meat is leaner than beef and has a richer flavor, making it both a healthy and tasty option.

Lobster Bisque

Serves: 1

INGREDIENTS:
- 150g lobster meat
- 2 cups lobster stock
- 1/4 cup heavy cream
- 1 tbsp butter
- Salt, pepper, and paprika to taste

STEPS:
In a pot, melt butter and sauté lobster meat until slightly colored.
Add lobster stock and bring to a simmer.
Stir in heavy cream, then season.
Serve hot, garnished with a sprinkle of paprika.

Fact: Lobster is not only decadent but also a great source of selenium and vitamin B12, both essential for neurological health.

Beef T-bone Steak

Serves: 1

INGREDIENTS:

- 1 T-bone steak (approx. 250g)
- 1 tbsp olive oil
- Salt and pepper to taste

STEPS:

Let the steak come to room temperature.
Preheat a skillet or grill. Season the steak generously.
Cook to your desired level of doneness.
Let rest for a few minutes before serving.

Fact: The T-bone steak combines two different textures and flavors with the tender fillet and the flavorful sirloin, offering a unique steak experience.

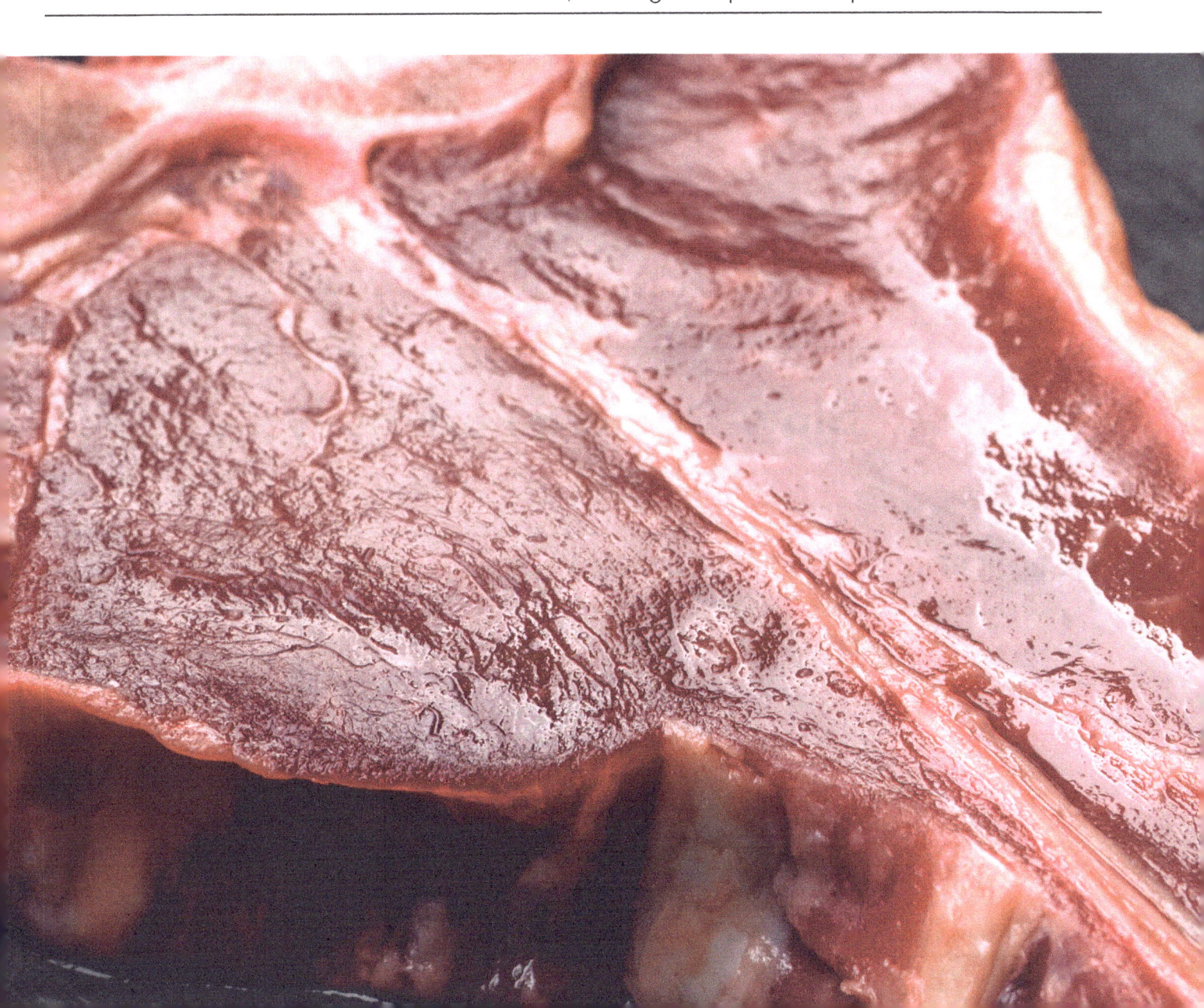

DAY 23

☀ **BREAKFAST** ☼ **LUNCH** ☾ **DINNER**

Ground Veal and Eggs

Serves: 1

INGREDIENTS:
- 100g ground veal
- 2 eggs
- 1 tbsp butter or ghee
- Salt and pepper to taste

STEPS:
In a skillet, cook ground veal in butter until browned.
Push meat to one side and scramble the eggs on the other.
Season and serve.

Fact: Veal is tender and has a milder flavor compared to beef, and it's rich in niacin and vitamin B6.

Slow-Cooked Pork Belly

Serves: 1

INGREDIENTS:
- 150g pork belly, skin scored
- 1 tsp olive oil
- Salt and pepper to taste

STEPS:
Preheat oven to 300°F (150°C).
Rub pork belly with oil, salt, and pepper.
Place in a roasting tray and bake for 2-3 hours or until tender and crispy.
Slice and serve.

Fact: Pork belly is a delightful mix of meat and fat, making it incredibly flavorful. It's also a good source of monounsaturated fats.

Grilled Eel with Butter

Serves: 1

INGREDIENTS:
- 1 eel fillet
- 1 tbsp butter
- Salt to taste
- Lemon wedge

STEPS:
Season the eel fillet.
Grill or broil until the skin crisps and the flesh is tender.
Serve with melted butter and a lemon wedge.

Fact: Eel is rich in omega-3 fatty acids and has a unique, buttery texture that's quite distinct from other fish.

DAY 24

☀ BREAKFAST ☼ LUNCH ☾ DINNER

Beef Hot Dogs with Scrambled Eggs

Serves: 1

INGREDIENTS:
- 2 beef hot dogs
- 2 eggs
- 1 tbsp butter or ghee
- Salt and pepper to taste

STEPS:
In a skillet, cook hot dogs in half of the butter until browned. In the same skillet, scramble eggs in the remaining butter. Season and serve together.

Fact: While many hot dogs contain fillers and additives, premium beef hot dogs offer a cleaner ingredient profile and taste.

Grilled Goose Breast

Serves: 1

INGREDIENTS:
- 1 goose breast (approx. 200g)
- 1 tbsp olive oil
- Salt, pepper, and rosemary to taste

STEPS:
Marinate the goose breast in olive oil, salt, pepper, and rosemary for at least 30 minutes. Grill over medium heat until medium rare or to desired doneness. Let rest for a few minutes, then slice and serve.

Fact: Goose meat is a rich, dark meat that's leaner than duck and has a bold flavor profile.

Mussels in Garlic Butter

Serves: 1

INGREDIENTS:

- 200g mussels, cleaned
- 2 garlic cloves, minced
- 2 tbsp butter
- Parsley and lemon wedge for garnish

STEPS:

In a pot, melt butter and sauté garlic until fragrant. Add mussels and cover. Cook until they open, about 5-7 minutes. Discard any that don't open. Serve hot with parsley and a squeeze of lemon.

Fact: Mussels are not only delicious but also a great source of essential minerals like zinc and selenium.

DAY 25

☀ BREAKFAST   ☼ LUNCH   ☾ DINNER

Beef Ham and Eggs

Serves: 1

INGREDIENTS:

- 2 slices beef ham
- 2 eggs
- 1 tbsp butter or ghee
- Salt and pepper to taste

STEPS:

In a skillet, cook beef ham slices until slightly browned.
Push ham to one side and fry the eggs on the other.
Season and serve.

Fact: Beef ham is a leaner alternative to pork ham but still offers a savory flavor profile.

Clams with Lemon Butter

Serves: 1

INGREDIENTS:

- 200g clams, cleaned
- 2 tbsp butter
- Zest and juice of 1/2 lemon
- Parsley for garnish

STEPS:

In a pot, melt butter and add lemon zest.
Add clams and cover. Cook until they open, about 5-7 minutes.
Add lemon juice. Discard any clams that don't open.
Garnish with parsley and serve.

Fact: Clams are an excellent source of vitamin B12, which is crucial for nerve function and the formation of red blood cells.

Roasted Quail

Serves: 1

INGREDIENTS:

- 1 whole quail, cleaned
- 1 tbsp olive oil
- Salt, pepper, and thyme to taste

STEPS:

Preheat the oven to 375°F (190°C).
Season duck leg with salt and pepper.
Roast in the oven for about 45 minutes or until skin is crispy and meat is cooked through.
Serve hot.

Fact: Quail is a delicacy known for its tender meat and is a good source of phosphorus, niacin, and zinc.

DAY 26

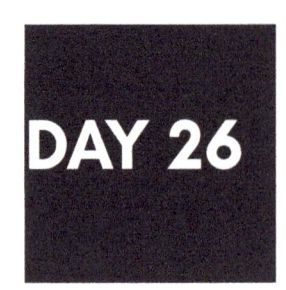

☀ BREAKFAST ☼ LUNCH ☾ DINNER

Ground Pork and Poached Eggs

Serves: 1

INGREDIENTS:
- 100g ground pork
- 2 eggs
- Salt and pepper to taste
- 1 tsp white vinegar (for poaching)

STEPS:

In a skillet, cook the ground pork until browned. Season to taste.

In a separate pot, bring water to a simmer and add vinegar.

Poach eggs until whites are set but yolks are runny.

Serve pork with poached eggs on top.

Fact: Pork is a versatile meat that is rich in thiamine, a vitamin that plays a crucial role in energy production and cell function.

Lamb Shoulder Roast

Serves: 1

INGREDIENTS:
- 200g lamb shoulder
- 1 tbsp olive oil
- Salt, pepper, and rosemary to taste

STEPS:

Preheat oven to 350°F (175°C).

Rub lamb shoulder with olive oil, salt, pepper, and rosemary.

Roast in the oven until tender, about 40-45 minutes.

Let rest, then slice and serve.

Fact: Lamb is rich in protein, vitamins, and minerals. It's particularly high in vitamin B12, iron, and zinc.

Grilled Tilapia with Olive Oil

Serves: 1

INGREDIENTS:

- 1 tilapia fillet
- 1 tbsp olive oil
- Salt and pepper to taste
- Lemon wedges for serving

STEPS:

Season the tilapia fillet with olive oil, salt, and pepper.
Grill over medium heat until cooked through.
Serve hot with lemon wedges.

Fact: Most popular in the Philippines

DAY 27

☀ BREAKFAST ☀ LUNCH ☾ DINNER

Duck Egg Omelette with Beef Strips

Serves: 1

INGREDIENTS:
- 2 duck eggs
- 100g beef strips
- 1 tbsp butter or ghee
- Salt and pepper to taste
- Fresh herbs (optional: parsley or chives)

STEPS:
In a bowl, whisk duck eggs with salt, pepper, and herbs.
Heat butter in a pan over medium heat.
Add beef strips and sauté until cooked to your liking.
Pour in the whisked eggs, stirring occasionally.
Cook until the omelette is set, then fold and serve hot.

Fact: Duck eggs are richer and have a larger yolk than chicken eggs, providing a creamier texture in dishes.

Grilled Lamb Koftas

Serves: 1

INGREDIENTS:
- 150g ground lamb
- 1 tsp cumin
- 1 tsp coriander
- Salt and pepper to taste

STEPS:
In a bowl, mix ground lamb with cumin, coriander, salt, and pepper.
Shape the mixture into elongated koftas around skewers.
Grill on medium heat until well-browned and cooked through.
Serve hot.

Fact: Lamb is a good source of omega-3 fats, known for their anti-inflammatory properties.

Pan-Seared Tuna with Butter Sauce

Serves: 1

INGREDIENTS:

- 1 tuna steak
- 2 tbsp butter
- 1 garlic clove, minced
- Juice of half a lemon
- Salt and pepper to taste

STEPS:

Season tuna steak with salt and pepper.

In a skillet, melt 1 tbsp butter and sear the tuna steak until it's cooked to your liking.

In a separate pan, melt the remaining butter, add minced garlic, and cook until fragrant.

Add lemon juice to the garlic butter sauce, stir, and pour over the tuna steak.

Serve immediately.

Fact: Tuna is an excellent source of high-quality protein and contains omega-3 fatty acids, which are good for heart health.

DAY 28

☀ BREAKFAST ☀ LUNCH ☾ DINNER

Veal Sausages with Eggs

Serves: 1

INGREDIENTS:
- 2 veal sausages
- 2 eggs
- Butter or ghee for frying
- Salt and pepper to taste

STEPS:
Proceed as in Day 27.

Fact: Eggs are among the most nutritious foodson the planet, containing a bit of almost every nutrient that our bodies need..

Beef Prime Rib

Serves: 1

INGREDIENTS:
- 200g beef prime rib
- 1 tbsp olive oil
- Salt and rosemary to taste

STEPS:
Preheat oven to 350°F (175°C).
Rub beef prime rib with olive oil, salt, and rosemary.
Roast in the oven until medium-rare or
to your preferred doneness.
Let rest, then slice and serve.

Fact: Prime rib is a cut of beef from the rib section, known for its rich flavor and tenderness.

Scallops with Butter and Lemon

Serves: 1

INGREDIENTS:

- 5-6 large scallops
- 1 tbsp butter
- Salt and pepper to taste
- Lemon wedges for serving

STEPS:

Preheat oven to 350°F (175°C).
Rub beef prime rib with olive oil, salt, and rosemary.
Roast in the oven until medium-rare or to your preferred doneness.
Let rest, then slice and serve.

Fact: Scallops are not only delicious but also packed with vitamin B12 and omega-3 fatty acids.

End of Week Reflection:
Celebrate and Cultivate - The Encore of Excellence

Physical Fitness Tip: Incorporating Flexibility and Balance Exercises

The Dance of Carnivores: Just as the carnivore diet has been about balancing various meats, your physical health can greatly benefit from a balance in muscle flexibility and core strength. Think of your body as a violin string. Too tight, and it might snap. Too loose, and it won't play. Yoga and pilates are fabulous ways to stretch those muscles and fortify your core. It's like adding the finishing touches to a masterpiece; these exercises ensure that your body remains as supple as it is strong.

Mental Shifts: Confidence Boost and a Sense of Accomplishment

The Lion's Roar: By now, you're not the same person who started this diet. Much like a lion who's discovered the vastness of its territory, you've explored new dietary horizons. The hesitations, the curiosity, and the commitment have all culminated in this moment of pride. You've tackled challenges, and now, there's this newfound confidence, almost like a lion's roar echoing through the savannah. Take a moment to pat yourself on the back; you've achieved something incredible!

Health Checkpoint: Acknowledging Overall Well-Being and Future Steps

The Health Horizon: Stand on the peak of this carnivore mountain you've climbed and look around. How do you feel? Lighter? Stronger? More alert? This is a time not just to reflect on the past weeks but to look at the horizon of your health journey. Your body might be giving you cues on what's working and what might need tweaking. This isn't the end but rather a checkpoint. Take notes, adjust if needed, and remember that health is an ever-evolving journey, much like the winding roads ahead. Buckle up and enjoy the ride!

YOUR 28-DAY CARNIVOROUS CHRONICLE

Reflecting on the 28-Day Journey

The Great Safari Adventure: Imagine having been on an epic safari through uncharted territories. There were wild sights, unexpected encounters, and yes, maybe a few bumps on the road. This carnivore journey has been similar – an expedition into the wild terrain of meat, fats, and proteins. There were times of doubt, perhaps, moments where the old foliage of previous diets beckoned. But you pressed on. Look back and marvel at the distance covered. You've discovered new things about your body, your willpower, and perhaps even the vast plains of the meat aisle!

Steps Forward After the 28 Days

Charting New Maps

Every seasoned explorer understands that the end of one trek only heralds the beginning of another. As the sun sets on this 28-day carnivore journey, a new horizon beckons. So, what's the next vista you'd like to venture into? Here are some ways to navigate your next dietary exploration:

Reflect & Reassess: Before you set sail again, take a moment to drop anchor and think. How did you feel on the carnivore diet? Was your energy consistent? Did you sleep well? Reflect on both the highs and the lows of your experience.

Blend & Balance: If you loved parts of the carnivore diet but missed certain food groups, consider creating a fusion menu. Merge the best bits of the carnivore diet with elements from paleo, keto, or Mediterranean diets.

Experiment & Experience: Use the upcoming weeks to try out new diets, or even variations within the carnivore spectrum itself. Different cuts of meat, new preparation methods, or integrating occasional plant-based days – the culinary world is vast and waiting!

Consult & Converse: Share your journey with friends or join online communities. Learn from their experiences and adapt suggestions that resonate with you. A fresh perspective often opens new avenues.

Educate & Evolve: Invest time in reading up or attending workshops about nutrition. A deeper understanding will help you craft a diet that's uniquely suited to your needs.

Listen & Learn: The most trustworthy guide you have is your own body. It whispers – sometimes shouts – its needs and preferences. Whether it's a craving, a sense of fullness, an energy surge, or a slump, keep an ear out for these signals. They're the breadcrumbs leading to your optimal diet.

Flexibility is the Spice of Dietary Life: Remember that rigidly sticking to a particular diet isn't necessary. The world of nutrition isn't black and white. If you feel like having a salad or a fruit bowl occasionally, it's okay. Being too strict can sometimes take the joy out of eating.

Tips for Maintaining a Balanced Carnivore Lifestyle

The Balanced Butcher: Variety is the spice of life. Keep exploring different cuts, animals, and even cooking methods to keep things exciting.
Hydration Station: Meat can be heavy. Ensure you're drinking enough water to help digestion and to stay hydrated.
Vitamin Ventures: Occasionally, you might want to incorporate organ meats or even supplements to ensure you're not missing out on essential nutrients.
Listening Lounge: Always, always tune into your body. If it's singing, dance along. If it's hinting at a tweak here or there, take heed.
Community Camp: Join online carnivore communities or local groups. Sharing recipes, stories, and experiences can be incredibly enriching.
In conclusion, every journey is about discovery – of the world and oneself. This 28-day carnivore quest was no different. As you move forward, take with you the lessons, the flavors, and the strength you've garnered. And remember, every meal, every choice, is a new step in the ever-evolving dance of health and happiness. Here's to many more steps, leaps, and bounds!

ANCIENT APPETITES:

The Meaty Melody of Yore:
Feasting on Fossils: Picture our hunter-gatherer ancestors, twiddling their primitive tools, plotting the day's hunt. The stakes? Not just bragging rights for the biggest mammoth catch but life itself! That carnivorous commitment wasn't just about taste—it was survival jazz in its purest form.

Hunter's Hootenanny: The thrill of the chase, the camaraderie among hunters, and the subsequent feast - it was the original block party! Meat didn't just fill bellies; it fortified bonds. Think of it as the prehistoric potluck, where the dish du jour was always meaty!

Pop Culture Parallel:
Paleo Party: Rocking up in our modern times, the paleo diet (with its "eat like your ancestors" mantra) gave a nod to our old-school dietary dances. The carnivore diet? Think of it as paleo's hardcore cousin who only grooves to meaty beats!

Modern Mavericks:
The Social Media Meat Market:
Tweeting the T-Bone: One post about a ribeye steak, and boom! Instant virality. The Internet's insatiable appetite for trends devoured personal anecdotes of carnivore conquests. From before-after selfies to juicy steak snaps, the web was awash in meaty tales.

Vlogging the Veal: Watch a YouTuber chronicle their 30-day carnivore challenge, and suddenly, you're knee-deep in the comment section at 2 am, debating the merits of grass-fed vs. grain-fed. Such is the power of the meaty matrix online!

Pop Culture Parallel:

Rogan's Ruminations: With powerhouses like Joe Rogan biting into the carnivore chat, the diet found its stage. When celebrities chewed the fat (literally and figuratively) on such diets, the masses listened, mused, and many, munching alongside!

Scientific Scrutiny:
Peeking Under the Prime Rib:
To Meat or Not to Meat: Every dietary diva has its day in the scientific sun. With the carnivore diet, it's a dance of duality. While some research serenades its benefits, others drop a more cautionary beat.

Quality Over Quantity: Not all meats make the same music. Grass-fed, wild-caught, organic - these aren't just hipster hashtags. They're the markers of quality that play a lead role in the carnivore concert.

Pop Culture Parallel:

Screen & Stream: "The Magic Pill," "What The Health," "Keto Explained" - modern media has a penchant for dietary docudramas. The carnivore chorus, albeit divisive, has woven its narrative into this ever-evolving cinematic soundtrack.

COUNTERCULTURE AND CURIOSITY:

The Vegan's Vexing Cousin:
Swinging the Dietary Pendulum: For every action, there's an equal and opposite reaction, right? As plant-based diets pushed forward, a meat-centric counter-movement swung back. The carnivore diet became the rebel with a cause (and a steak)!
A Tale of Two Extremes: Vegan or Carnivore? It's like the Beatles vs. the Rolling Stones of dietary debates. But hey, whether you're team tofu or team T-bone, it's all part of the rich tapestry of culinary choices.

Pop Culture Parallel:
Eat, Pray, Post: Social platforms became the battleground for dietary debates. Carnivore enthusiasts and critics alike turned to memes, posts, and stories to stake their culinary claims, making meat-eating as much a social statement as a personal preference.

The Carnivore on a Budget: Making Meaty Moves Without Emptying the Wallet

1. Buy in Bulk: The Harmonic Hack: Like a beautiful chorus, buying in bulk can mean harmony for your finances. Purchasing larger quantities often results in per-pound savings. Consider investing in a deep freezer to store surplus.
US: Many warehouse clubs like Costco or Sam's Club offer deals on bulk meats.
UK: Bulk-buying websites or wholesalers like Bookers can be a lifesaver.
AUS: Australian Bulk Foods or stores like Costco offer similar deals.

2. Choose Less Expensive Cuts: The Beat of Bargain: Not all cuts are born equal. Opt for chuck roast, pork shoulder, or chicken thighs instead of premium cuts. They might take a tad longer to cook, but they're equally delightful.
US: Ground beef, pork butt, and chicken legs can be more affordable.
UK: Minced beef, pork belly, and lamb neck can be economical choices.
AUS: Beef mince, lamb flaps, or chicken drumsticks can be pocket-friendly.

3. Embrace Organ Meats: The Offbeat Octave: They're not everyone's first choice, but organ meats like liver, heart, or kidneys are nutrient-dense and often cheaper.
US: Check out local butcher shops or farmers markets for a variety of offal.
UK: Local butchers or even supermarkets like Tesco offer a range of organ meats.
AUS: Specialty butchers or even Woolworths might have a good selection of offal.

4. Shop Sales and Seasonal Specials: The Seasonal Symphony: Timing is everything. Buy meat when it's on sale, and if possible, during seasonal offers.
US: Holidays like the 4th of July or Memorial Day often come with meat sales.
UK: Post-Christmas or during BBQ season, stores like ASDA or Sainsbury's might have deals.
AUS: Around Australia Day or Easter, you might find offers in Coles or Aldi.

5. Consider Direct Purchases: The Direct Drumbeat: Bypassing the middleman by buying directly from farmers can lead to fresh meat at a fraction of the price.
US: Websites like EatWild can connect you with local farmers.
UK: Direct meat suppliers like Farmison & Co offer delivery services.
AUS: Farmhouse Direct is a platform connecting consumers with Aussie producers.

6. Get Creative with Leftovers: The Recycled Rhythm: Think bone broths, stews, or even meaty salads. Using every bit ensures nothing goes to waste.
US: Bone broths are trendy and can be made from leftover bones.
UK: Traditional stews or pies can incorporate leftover meats.
AUS: Meat pies or slow-cooked recipes can be a haven for remains.

7. Be Wary of Import Costs: The Import Interlude: Local is often more affordable than imported due to taxes and transportation costs.
US: Domestic beef or poultry might be more affordable than imports.
UK: Opt for British beef or lamb to potentially save more.
AUS: Australian beef or kangaroo meat could be more cost-effective than imported options.
Like a maestro leading an orchestra, lead your budget with finesse and intelligence. With a bit of research, creativity, and strategy, the carnivore diet can be both a delightful and affordable tune.
Use this tracker every day during your carnivore journey to monitor your emotional and physical reactions to the diet. By the end of 28 days, this will give you a comprehensive overview of how the carnivore diet resonated with you.

**Join us on your favorite platform.
Scan the Qr code on your phone or tablet**

Made in the USA
Las Vegas, NV
13 November 2023